MAKING MAGIC

If you enjoy MAKING MAGIC — then this is the book for you . . .

Every trick is fully illustrated with step-by-step instructions and there are tricky tips and jokes to make even a beginner a master magician.

3 bcd

MAKING MAGIC
A CAROUSEL BOOK 0 552 54114 1

First publication in Great Britain

PRINTING HISTORY
Carousel edition published 1976

Carousel Books are published by Transworld Publishers Ltd
Century House 61-63 Uxbridge Road, Ealing W5 56A.

Made and printed in Great Britain by the Guernsey Press Co. Ltd., Guernsey,
Channel Islands.

MAKING MAGIC

Malcolm Carrick

Illustrated by the author

CAROUSEL BOOKS
A DIVISION OF TRANSWORLD PUBLISHERS LTD

TRiCKY TiPS!

WHENEVER YOU WANT TO SLiP SOMETHING iN OR OUT OF ONE HAND, WAVE AND POINT THE OTHER TO "MiS-DIRECT" THE AUDIENCE.

DON'T LET YOUR AUDIENCE TOO CLOSE TO THE TRICKS.(iN CASE THEY SEE THREADS AND STUFF).

HAVE YOUR PROPS OUT OF SiGHT UNTIL NEEDED

EDiBLE PROPS

NOW, BEFORE MY NEXT TRICK WITH THIS ORDINARY CANDLE AND MY NEW WAND, I MUST EAT SOMETHING.

NO FOOD ABOUT, SO I EAT THE CANDLE, YUMMY

AND, AS I'M STILL PECKISH, I'LL EAT MY WAND!

HOW'S IT DONE?

THE TOP PART OF THE CANDLE IS REALLY A CUT-OUT SECTION OF APPLE, HELD TO THE CANDLE BY A MATCHSTICK

THE WICK IS A PIECE OF ALMOND

MY WAND IS A STICK OF LICORICE

THE WHITE ENDS ARE MADE OF ICING SUGAR MIXED INTO A PASTE WITH WATER

DO THESE JOKES BEFORE THE OTHER TRICKS, THE AUDIENCE WILL EAT FROM YOUR HAND

MAGIC BAG

AN EMPTY PAPER-BAG.

WITH MY RIGHT HAND I FLICK AN IMAGINARY COIN UP INTO THE AIR.

AND IT LANDS IN THE BAG WITH A THUMP

INSIDE, THERE'S A REAL COIN

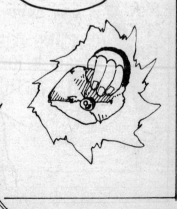

HOW TO DO IT

WHEN EVERYONE IS LOOKING AT THE 'PRETEND' COIN, I DROP THE REAL COIN INTO THE BAG

THE REAL COIN IS HIDDEN BETWEEN MY FINGERS HOLDING THE BAG.

WHEN THE 'PRETEND' COIN LANDS, I CLICK MY 3RD FINGER AGAINST THE SIDE OF THE BAG

SO, IT'S 3RD FINGER OVER 2ND FINGER, PRESS; THEN LET YOUR 3RD FINGER HIT THE BAG.

FRENCH DROP

HOW'S IT DONE?

IT NEVER LEFT MY LEFT HAND, WHEN I CLENCH MY RIGHT HAND OVER MY LEFT...

I DROP THE COIN INTO MY LEFT PALM .....

THEN, CLENCH MY LEFT HAND AROUND THE COIN. IF YOU POINT AT YOUR RIGHT HAND YOU MIS-DIRECT PEOPLE INTO THINKING THE COIN IS THERE.

PAPER TEARING

I MAKE TWO TEARS IN A SHEET OF NEWSPAPER

AND ASK A FRIEND TO TRY TO TEAR THE PAPER INTO **THREE** SECTIONS

HE CANNOT DO IT TRICKSTERS, HOW TEARFUL HA, HA.

STOOGE

HERES A TRICK FOR A PARTY

ASK SOMEONE TO PUT A WALNUT OR A MARBLE UNDER ONE OF 3 CUPS

YOU LEAVE THE ROOM WHILE THEY DO IT

YOU RETURN, AND STRAIGHTAWAY CHOOSE THE RIGHT ONE

HOW'S IT DONE?

SIMPLE IN THE ROOM IS MY STOOGE WHO SEES WHICH

CUP THE WALNUT IS UNDER AND **COUGHS**

ONCE TWICE THREE TIMES

HERE'S ANOTHER ONE TO DRIVE THEM NUTS!

ASK SOMEONE TO PLACE ANY COIN UNDER A MUG.

WHILE YOU LEAVE THE ROOM

YOU RETURN AND AT ONCE TELL THE VALUE OF THE COIN UNDER THE MUG.

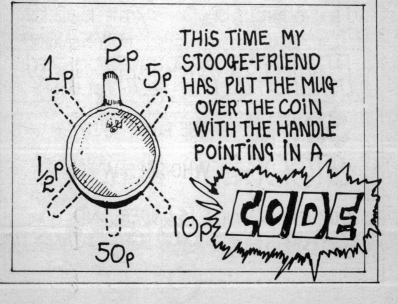

THIS TIME MY STOOGE-FRIEND HAS PUT THE MUG OVER THE COIN WITH THE HANDLE POINTING IN A

CODE

1p   2p   5p

½p

10p

50p

MOVING PENCIL

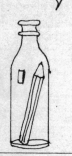

HOW'S IT DONE?

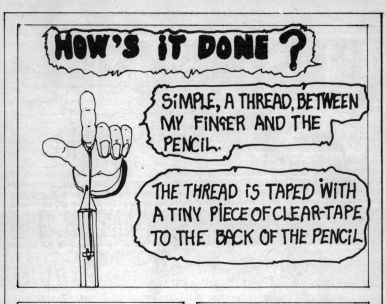

SIMPLE, A THREAD, BETWEEN MY FINGER AND THE PENCIL.

THE THREAD IS TAPED WITH A TINY PIECE OF CLEAR-TAPE TO THE BACK OF THE PENCIL

WHEN I TAKE THE PENCIL OUT OF THE BOTTLE, I PULL THE THREAD OFF. HO HO

TRY THE SAME IDEA WITH THE THREAD TAPED UNDER A COIN.

REMEMBER, THE THIN THREAD MUST BE THE SAME COLOUR AS THE BACK-GROUND

RISING COIN

HERE IS A DRAWER-TYPE CIGARETTE PACKET

AND A COIN **5**p

ANY COIN WILL DO

I PUT THE COIN IN AT THE BOTTOM, AND TAP HARD ON THE TOP

THE COIN RISES UP THROUGH THE PACKET!!!!!!!

WHY?

BECAUSE WHEN YOU TAP HARD, THE BOX IS JOLTED DOWN, WHILE THE COIN STAYS STILL.

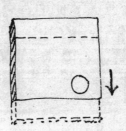

THE PACKET MUST BE NEARLY FULL, IF NOT WITH CIGARETTES THEN.,...

..USE PAPER TO FILL IT

THE COIN 90ES HERE TRICKSTERS

MIND READING

 I HAVE AN ENVELOPE HERE WHICH I GIVE TO A MEMBER OF THE AUDIENCE

NOW I READ THE MIND

 I WANT YOU TO THINK OF A FAMOUS PERSON

CHARLIE CHAPLIN

NOW OPEN THE ENVELOPE, AND YOU WILL FIND A PHOTO OF CHARLIE CHAPLIN

WHEN HE WAS A BABY HA, HA!

ANY BABY-PHOTO WILL DO, BECAUSE THEY ALL LOOK MUCH THE SAME

PLAYING with CARDS

WHERE DOES IT COME FROM?

HOW'S IT DONE?

COLOUR CHANGE!

AND IT CHANGES COLOUR

HOW'S IT DONE?

THE PENCIL HAS A DIFFERENT COLOURED PAPER ROLL AROUND IT.

GLUED.

WHEN I 'WIPE' THE PENCIL . I HOLD THE POINT. AND TAKE OFF THE PAPER ROLL, INSIDE THE HANKY.

ALL YOU NEED. MAKE THE FAKE BY ROLLING THE STRIP OF PAPER TIGHTLY AROUND THE PENCIL AND GLUE IT.

IT'S SURE TO DRAW THE CROWDS HA, HA

FIND THE JOKER

A PAPER CLIP

(DON'T GET IT ROUND THE EAR, HO, HO)

MY ASSISTANT WILL NOW PLACE THE CLIP ON THE BACK OF THE JOKER.

AND WE ALL SAY THE MAGIC WORD

CAROUSEL

I TURN THE CARDS OVER, AND THE JOKER HAS MOVED

TURN THE CARDS OVER AND THE CLIP IS STILL IN THE SAME PLACE

HOW IT'S DONE.

NO TRICK AT ALL.

PAPER LOOPS

2 LONG STRIPS OF NEWSPAPER

I GLUE THEM INTO 2 LOOPS

I GIVE ONE TO A FRIEND, AND ASK HIM TO CUT IT THROUGH THE CENTRE.

I DO THE SAME, MY LOOP GOES INTO ONE LARGE ONE, BUT MY FRIEND'S IS JUST CUT IN TWO.

HOW'S IT DONE?

I DO IT AGAIN, THIS TIME, MY LOOPS ARE INSIDE EACH OTHER

BEFORE I STUCK MY FIRST LOOP, I PUT ONE **TWIST** IN THE NEWSPAPER.

FOR INTERLOCKING LOOPS PUT **2** TWISTS IN THE NEWSPAPER BEFORE STICKING.

KEEP THE TWISTS A SECRET!

LONG CARD

HOW'S IT DONE?

I'VE ALREADY PUT ALL THE NUMBERED CLUBS (1-10) IN THE CENTRE OF THE PACK.

NOW I HOLD MY THUMBS OVER THE OTHER CARDS, SO ONLY A CLUB CARD CAN BE TAKEN.

TO MAKE THE LONG CARD, STICK 10 'CLUB' PIPS ON A STRIP OF PAPER ROLL IT UP IN YOUR POCKET.

AND JUST KEEP PULLING IT OUT UNTIL YOU REACH THE RIGHT NUMBER *HEE HEE!*

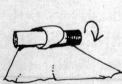

DISAPPEARING MILK

TWO EMPTY GLASSES AND A JUG OF MILK

I COVER UP ONE GLASS AND FILL THE OTHER WITH MILK.

I UNCOVER THE 2ND GLASS, AND FIND IT HAS FILLED BY ITSELF.

I COVER IT AGAIN THEN EMPTY THE 1ST GLASS

I UNCOVER THE 2ND GLASS AND FIND IT HAS EMPTIED BY ITSELF!

HOW'S IT DONE?

THE 2ND "GLASS OF MILK" IS REALLY JUST A SHEET OF PAPER, CUT TO EXACTLY THE SIZE OF THE GLASS AND ROLLED INSIDE IT.

TO "FILL" THE GLASS, I PUT THE PAPER IN IT, UNDER COVER FROM THE CLOTH.

TO "EMPTY" IT, I TAKE THE PAPER OUT IN THE CLOTH

SPOTTED IT?

CUT OUT A PIECE OF CARD, THE SIZE OF A PLAYING-CARD, THEN STICK **7** RED PAPER DIAMONDS ON, LIKE THIS.....

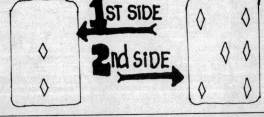

THE SECRET IS HOW YOU HOLD THE CARD WHEN YOU TURN IT OVER.

1ST SIDE

FOR AN ACE

FOR A **3**

2ND SIDE

FOR A. **4**

FOR A **5**

FOR A **7**

TURN ROUND

CUT 2 PIECES OF PAPER (ABOUT THE SIZE OF A £1 NOTE)

PAINT ONE BLACK AND ONE WHITE.

NOW FIND A **PENCIL.**

I PLACE THE BLACK PAPER, LENGTHWAYS UNDER THE WHITE.

NOW ROLL THEM BOTH AROUND THE PENCIL.

NOW I SAY THE MAGIC WORD

CAROUSEL

AND UNROLL THE PAPER AND....

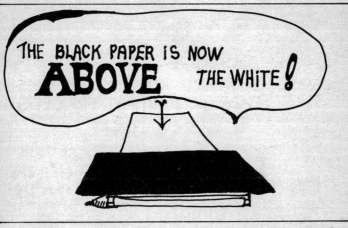

THE BLACK PAPER IS NOW **ABOVE** THE WHITE!

ANY DIFFERENT COLOURED PAPERS WILL DO TRICKSTERS, IF YOU'RE RICH, TRY IT WITH A £1 AND A £5 NOTE A WEALTH OF FUN, TEE HEE!

PAPER CLIPS

2 PAPER CLIPS

AND A STRIP OF PAPER

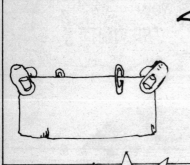

I FOLD THE PAPER, AND PUT THE CLIPS ON IT.
THEY ARE FAR A-PART, LIKE THE POSH ACTOR HA!

NOW WITH MAGIC I PULL THE PAPER, AND THE CLIPS JUMP UP JOINED

HOW TO DO IT

FOLD THE PAPER LIKE THIS

PUT THE FIRST CLIP OVER THESE TWO EDGES

AND THE 2ND CLIP OVER THESE TWO

NOW JUST **PULL**

DON'T LET YOUR FRIENDS SEE WHERE YOU PLACED THE CLIPS. ASK THEM TO TRY.

TRY IT WITH 2 CLIPS ON EACH SIDE

OR 3

MAGIC THREAD

I FILL A GLASS WITH WATER, AND POP IN, AN ICE CUBE

HERE IS AN ORDINARY LENGTH OF COTTON

WITHOUT LOOPS OR KNOTS, HOW CAN THE CUBE BE LIFTED ?

I PUT **MAGIC** ON THE COTTON.

THE ICE-CUBE NOW STICKS TO THE COTTON !!!

HOW TO DO IT

WHILE EVERYONE IS LOOKING AT THE COTTON, I SPRINKLE A BIT OF **SALT.** ONTO THE ICE-CUBE.

THE SALT STICKS THE COTTON TO THE ICE

EXPERIMENT TO SEE HOW MUCH SALT YOU NEED; A PINCH SHOULD DO, HA,HA

ASK YOUR TEACHER WHY, IT WORKS

HOW'S IT DONE?

THE OPPOSITE SIDES OF A DICE ALWAYS ADD UP TO 7

IT DOESN'T MATTER iF PEOPLE KNOW THIS, BECAUSE THEY WILL NOT EXPECT A CARD WITH **14** ON IT.

COLOUR A PiECE OF PAPER **RED.**

THEN CUT OUT 14 DIAMONDS.

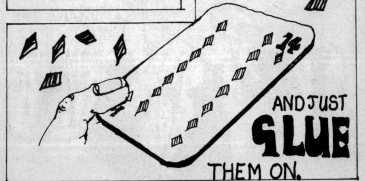

AND JUST **GLUE** THEM ON.

BALLOONS

HERE WE HAVE AN ORDINARY BALLOON

AND A PIN

IF YOU PIERCE THE BALLOON... IT GOES... POP

BUT WITH MAGIC

HOW'S IT DONE?

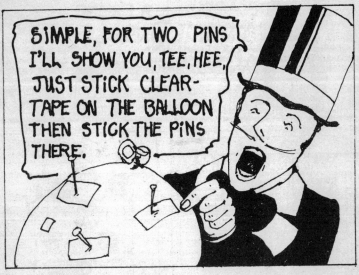

BOX OF TRICKS.

GET A LARGE CARDBOARD BOX FROM A SUPER-MARKET

BIG ENOUGH TO GET A FRIEND INSIDE

MAKE A 'TABLE-CLOTH' FOR THE BOX, BY PAINTING A NEWS-PAPER WITH LARGE BLACK SPOTS

CUT THE MIDDLE SPOT OUT

CUT OUT A HOLE IN THE BOX-TOP, THAT WILL MATCH THE ONE IN THE PAPER

AND CAROUSEL

NOW YOU CAN'T SEE THE HOLE, HEE, HEE.

BOTTLE & GLASS

THIRSTY WORK BEING A MAGICIAN

SO, I PICK UP AN ORDINARY BOTTLE OF MILK AND A CUP.

POUR MYSELF A SPLASH!

NOW I SCRATCH MY NOSE AND THE CUP STAYS IN MID AIR?

THAT'S BETTER, NOW I FINISH THE DROP OF MILK.

HOW'S IT DONE?

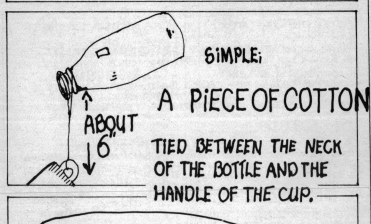

SIMPLE:

A PIECE OF COTTON

ABOUT ↑ ↓ 6"

TIED BETWEEN THE NECK OF THE BOTTLE AND THE HANDLE OF THE CUP.

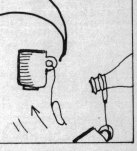

THIS LONG LOOP AROUND THE NECK OF THE BOTTLE, ENABLES YOU TO SEPARATE THEM EASILY.

REMEMBER, AS ALWAYS TRICKSTERS, THE THREAD MUST BE THE SAME COLOUR AS ITS SURROUNDINGS, IN THIS CASE, WHITE, OR A THIN NYLON THREAD IS BEST.

LETTERS

FIND SOME TRACING PAPER, OR SEE THROUGH KITCHEN FILM.

WRITE LOTS OF THINGS ON IT, INCLUDING

WOW

NOW TURN IT OVER. WOW IS STILL SPELT THE SAME WAY!

WHY? BECAUSE THESE LETTERS ARE SHAPED THE SAME WAY LEFT OR RIGHT.

AND THESE ARE THE SAME SHAPE FROM THE TOP OR BOTTOM SO THEY READ THE SAME IN A MIRROR.

FLOATING CARD

AN ORDINARY COTTON-REEL AND A PLAYING-CARD.

I ASK MY FRIEND TO BLOW THROUGH THE HOLE, AT THE CARD

HIS CARD BLOWS AWAY

BUT WHEN I DO THE SAME

CAROUSEL

THE CARD STICKS TO THE COTTON-REEL

HOW'S IT DONE?

WHEN I PICK UP THE CARD, MY FRIEND
HAS BLOWN OFF THE TABLE,
I STICK A PIN THROUGH IT.

(IN THE CENTRE)

THE PIN KEEPS THE CARD STUCK
TO THE COTTON-REEL WHILE YOU
BLOW

AS SOON AS YOU
STOP BLOWING,
GRAB THE CARD
SO NO-ONE SEES
THE PIN.

TAKE OUT THE PIN AND ASK THEM TO
TRY AGAIN, THAT WILL **NEEDLE** THEM
HO HO HO!

CAN'T BE DONE

DO YOU KNOW ANYONE WHO THINKS THEY ARE VERY STRONG?

TRY THIS ON THEM TIE A HEAVY BOOK IN A LONG PIECE OF STRING.

NOW ASK THEM TO PULL THE STRING INTO A HORIZONTAL POSITION. THEY MUST HOLD THEIR ARMS LIKE THIS

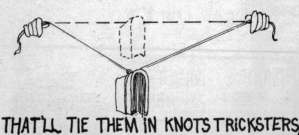

THAT'LL TIE THEM IN KNOTS TRICKSTERS

¡IT CAN'T BE DONE!

PENNY THROUGH PLATE

AN ORDINARY
PLATE, AND
A GLASS.

A SMALL COIN:
WHICH I PLACE
IN AN ENVELOPE.

I PLACE THE ENVELOPE ON
THE PLATE, TAP IT WITH
MY MAGIC WAND, AND...

THE PENNY GOES INTO
THE GLASS, **THROUGH
THE PLATE!**

AND THE
ENVELOPE'S
EMPTY
TRICKSTERS

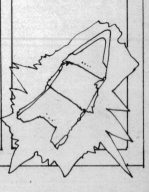

HOW'S IT DONE?

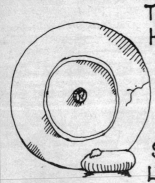

THE PLATE ALREADY HAS A COIN STUCK ON ITS UNDERSIDE. THE SHARP TAP OF THE WAND DISLODGES IT.

STICK IT ON WITH A LITTLE BIT OF SOAP.

THE OTHER COIN? I DROP IT IN MY LAP, IT NEVER WENT INTO THE ENVELOPE.

PRACTISE GETTING THE RIGHT AMOUNT OF SOAP, IF THE COIN DOESN'T DROP 1ST TIME, TAP AGAIN. ABOVE WHERE YOU KNOW IT IS.

FOO-CAN

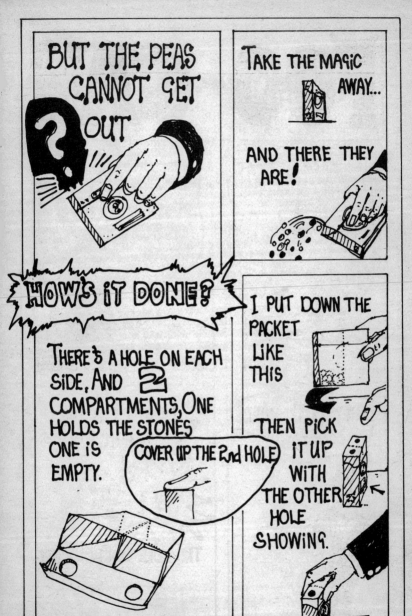

MICHAEL BENTINE'S POTTY ADVENTURE BOOK

0 552 52060 8   40p

You can join the Potties as they set off in their time box to visit the old Wild West to see how good Wild Bill Hiccup really was with his gun.

You can travel back in history with Professor Crankpotts from Pottisdam University to discover how the 'lump of stone' really found its way to Westminster Abbey, underneath the Coronation Chair.

You can join Colonel 'Potty' Potterton and his 19th Pottistani Lancers as they hold the Gateway to India against the yelling hordes of the Mad Mullah.

MALCOLM SAVILLE'S COUNTRY BOOK

0 552 54030 7   30p

It is not necessary to go far into the countryside to find a whole new world awaiting exploration. Malcolm Saville tells you how to gain the most from a day at the farm, a quiet browse by a pond, or a stroll along the hedgerows or through a wood — and stresses that there is much to be found all the year round.

He also tells you how to recognize the wild flowers and trees of the countryside, to distinguish between the barley and the oats in the farmers' fields and to recognise the snuffling of a hedgehog. You will discover how much extra enjoyment can be had on a walk by using a compass or a map, how to picnic and how to camp, and even how to recognize the stars at night.

EAT WHAT YOU GROW by Malcolm Saville

0 552 54075 7   30p

Have you ever eaten home-grown vegetables? They are delicious and don't necessarily need a lot of room. You can grow ridge cucumbers that start off in an egg box on a window ledge and mustard and cress which grows well on a flannel. You'll find many useful tips in this book.